Newspapers are printed on machines called presses

FIELD TRIPS

A Newspaper

Melissa Gish

A⁺

Smart Apple Media

COPYRIGHT

Published by Smart Apple Media

1980 Lookout Drive, North Mankato, MN 56003

Designed by Rita Marshall

Copyright © 2004 Smart Apple Media. International copyright reserved in all countries. No part of this book may be reproduced in any form without written permission from the publisher.

Printed in the United States of America

Photographs by The Image Finders (Mark E. Gibson), Tom Myers, Tom Stack & Associates (Brian Parker, Tom & Therisa Stack)

Library of Congress Cataloging-in-Publication Data

Gish, Melissa. A newspaper / by Melissa Gish.

p. cm. – (Field trips) Includes bibliographical references and index.

Summary: Introduces what a newsroom is like, who the people are that work to produce a newspaper, and how a paper is put together, printed, and delivered.

ISBN 1-58340-324-8

1. Newspaper publishing–Juvenile literature. 2. Journalism–Juvenile literature. [1. Newspaper publishing. 2. Journalism.] I. Title. II. Field trips (Smart Apple Media) (Mankato, Minn.).

PN4776.G57 2003   070.5'722–dc21   2002042787

First Edition 9 8 7 6 5 4 3 2 1

A Newspaper

CONTENTS

The Newsroom

Does your family have a newspaper delivered right to your own doorstep? Many people do. They learn what is happening in their towns and around the world from newspapers. Thousands of newspapers are published all over North America. Small-town newspapers may be printed weekly. In big cities the **presses** roll every day. A large newspaper may be open 24 hours a day because news is happening all the time. The newsroom, where the newspaper

Some dogs are trained to bring in the morning paper

is written, is a busy place. Large clocks remind workers that strict **deadlines** must be met. Telephones ring and computers click and beep. The **wire service** pumps out news in a steady stream. It requires teamwork to publish a newspaper. People must do their jobs quickly and correctly to get the newspaper written, printed, and delivered to the public before the news gets old!

The first daily newspaper in the United States was printed in 1783 to spread news about the new American government.

TV screens keep reporters informed as they work

Machines fold the pages of each newspaper together

Filling the Newspaper

The newspaper starts with reporters, people who gather news. They watch things happen, talk to people, and get the facts. When reporters gather enough information, they write news stories. These stories are given to editors. An editor's job is to read a news story to make sure it has

A byline appears under a headline. It tells the name of the reporter who wrote the article.

all the facts. The editor may also add or cut words from the story to make sure it fits in the newspaper. The editor-in-chief decides which stories to include and where they will appear in

the newspaper. The most important stories are put on the front

page. 🌀 Photographers may go with reporters to take

pictures for the newspaper. The photographs are given to the

A newspaper reporter takes notes for a news story

photo editor. This kind of editor decides which pictures will be used in the newspaper. The photo editor must check every photograph to pick the most clear and interesting. ∞ The paste-up artist makes all of the news stories, headlines, pictures, and **advertisements** fit into the space of the newspaper's pages. This isn't always easy. If there isn't enough space, the paste-up artist must ask the editor-in-chief to move stories to the next day's newspaper. Some stories may be dropped altogether.

It takes almost 500 tons (450 t) of paper to print *The New York Times* each day.

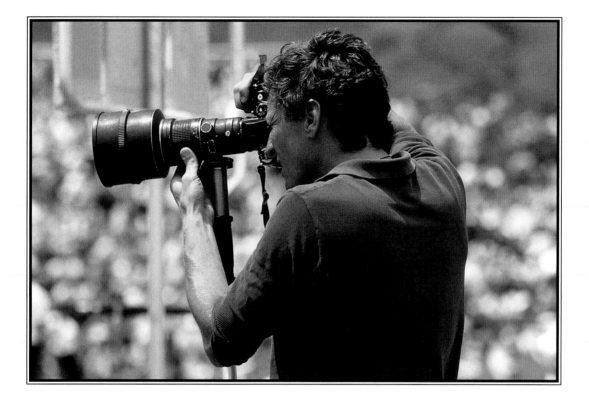

Going to Press

Reporters and editors use computers to work on news

stories. When the stories are ready, they are sent to a machine

Photographers report the news through pictures

that changes the typed stories into the right size and shape for a newspaper. The next stop is the composing room. Here people paste the stories and pictures onto big sheets of white cardboard. These boards will be sent to the platemaking room. Special lights are used to copy the images from the boards onto plates. Plates are thin sheets of plastic that are used to print the newspaper. Each letter and picture is burned on the plastic sheets. When ink is put on the plate, the ink will

Large presses can print 40,000 copies of a 96-page newspaper every hour.

Printing plates are mounted on rollers in the presses

stick only to the letters and pictures. ❧ The plates are sent

to the printing department. Huge printing presses fill entire

rooms and make lots of noise. The plates are attached to rollers

inside the printing press. Ink rollers spread ink onto the plates.

The inked plates roll across blankets. Blankets are rubbery

rollers that transfer ink from the plates to the paper. Heavy

rolls of paper, called newsprint, unwind through the blankets

of the printing press. The paper then goes through a dryer and

a cutter. The printed, cut paper is gathered and folded into

finished newspapers.

Extra! Extra!

A saying in the news business is, "Old news is no news." Newspapers have to get news out to readers quickly.

Long rolls of paper are printed and cut into pages

Often, a news story must go from the reporter all the way to the printer in only a few hours. Because the deadline is on everyone's mind, there is no room for mistakes at a newspaper.

Once the news has been printed in the newspaper, some of the newspapers are bundled and delivered by truck to stores and newsstands. People who **subscribe** to newspapers will have the papers mailed to them or delivered to their homes. By this time at a busy newspaper, work on the next day's edition has already begun.

A large newspaper may print 500,000 copies a day

Newspaper Paste-Up

Paste-up artists must do a lot of arranging and rearranging to make a newspaper fit together. Today, they have the help of computers, but it can still be difficult to arrange the news stories, pictures, and advertisements on a page in a short amount of time. To see just how tough it can be, try this activity.

What You Need

An old newspaper
Scissors

What You Do

1. Cut out all of the individual stories, pictures, and ads from two pages of the newspaper. Shuffle all of these pieces into a pile.
2. Open two new pages of the newspaper. Lay the pages flat on a table or the floor.
3. Arrange your cut-out pieces on top of the two new pages. Your goal is to make all the pieces fit without any empty spaces and without any extra pieces left over.

Headlines, pictures, articles, and ads fill up every page

INFORMATION

Index

Words to Know

advertisements (AD-vur-TYZ-mentz)—announcements that people pay money to
print in a newspaper

deadlines (DED-lynz)—times or dates by which things must be done

headline (HED-lyn)—words above a newspaper article that announce the topic

presses (PRESS-ez)—huge machines that print and fold newspapers

subscribe (SUB-skryb)—to pay for regular delivery of a newspaper

wire service (WYR SUR-vis)—a group that sends world news to newspapers

Read More

Bentley, Nancy. *The Young Journalists Book: How to Write and Produce Your Own
Newspaper.* Brookfield, Conn.: Millbrook Press, 2000.

Englart, Mindi Rose. *Newspapers: From Start to Finish.* Farmington Hills, Mich.:
Gale Group, 2001.

Oxlade, Chris. *Newspapers.* Crystal Lake, Ill.: Heinemann Library, 2001.

Internet Sites

A Brief History of Newspapers
http://www.historicpages.com/nprhist.htm

The New York Times
http://www.nytimes.com

CRAYON: Create Your Own
Newspaper Online
http://www.crayon.net/

Virtual Museum of the Printing Press
http://www.imultimedia.pt/
museuvirtpress/index_i.html